MY GAY MIDDLE AGES

MY GAY MIDDLE AGES

A.W. Strouse

punctum books * brooklyn, ny

MY GAY MIDDLE AGES
© A.W. Strouse, 2015.

First published in 2015 by
punctum books
Brooklyn, New York
http://punctumbooks.com

punctum books is an independent, open-access publisher dedicated to radically creative modes of intellectual inquiry and writing across a whimsical para-humanities assemblage. We solicit and pimp quixotic, sagely mad engagements with textual thought-bodies, and provide shelters for intellectual vagabonds.

The author wishes to thank Eileen A. Joy for supporting this project and Lauren Nickou for editorial help.

Cover Image: Nicolas Régnier, *St Sebastian* (c. 1620), Hermitage Museum, Russia.

ISBN-13: 978-0615830001
ISBN-10: 0615830005

Before you start to read this book, take this moment to think about making a donation to punctum books, an independent non-profit press,

@ http://punctumbooks.com/about/

If you're reading the e-book, you can click on the image below to go directly to our donations site. Any amount, no matter the size, is appreciated and will help us to keep our ship of fools afloat. Contributions from dedicated readers will also help us to keep our commons open and to cultivate new work that can't find a welcoming port elsewhere. Our adventure is not possible without your support. Vive la open-access.

Fig. 1. Hieronymous Bosch, *Ship of Fools* (1490-1500)

for J.H.

TABLE OF CONTENTS

Chapter 1

The Most Famous Medievalist in the World

I grew up in a small town in Pennsylvania, with a population of maybe 800 people.

The town was home to the biggest pile of used tires, east of the Mississippi.

A gentleman by the name of Maxwell Moon had been sold the tires.

He got paid like ten cents a tire, to store them.

After a few million tires, that really added up.

All of the tires he put on the side of a mountain.

From miles away there was this mountain, all covered in black, like Mordor.

The mountain was nothing but tires, and mosquitoes, and a few bloated old ponies that ate the grass that grew up between the tires.

It was like a dystopian Chincoteague.

After he'd been paid all that money to give a home to the tires, then Maxwell Starr used his new capital to start a Port-a-Potty company.

It was the most successful business in town.

He had turned excrement into gold, and then back into excrement—a real alchemist.

The port-a-potty factory was down by the creek, which was called Little Fishing Creek.

The town was founded by Quakers, who think that it's a sin to name places after people, because it's vain and arrogant.

Hence, they called the creek the Little Fishing Creek.

And the town was named Millville, after the gristmill, which formerly had been the most successful business in town, in the 17th century.

Pennsylvania was founded by William Penn, a Quaker, but he named the colony after his *father*, rather than after himself, and his father wasn't a Quaker, so that was a loophole.

Used tires and portable toilets are Pennsylvania's main sources of employment.

Pretty soon, someone ruined another mountain in our town by turning it into a landfill.

And then the oil companies came in, and started fracking.

Now it's really a neoliberal wasteland, but to me it will always be "home."

Although I moved to New York City, I still like Millville.

It was so small that everyone who lived there knew you.

They knew all of your business, and they knew all of your cousins.

Small towns are where anyone can be famous.

When I moved to New York City, suddenly I went from being famous to being a nobody, because in New York City there are ten million people and nobody knows anybody.

But after ten years in New York, I started to become famous in my own way.

After a certain point I realized that New York is also a very small town, or at least New York is made up of many small towns.

For example there is the "Art World," which is by itself a community of a few thousand people.

And there are the Williamsburg hipster kids—lots of them, but not so many that you can't get to know them.

So you can easily be famous to a small group of New Yorkers, the way you could be famous in Millville.

Of course many people move to New York so that they can "make it"—so that they can become world-famous superstars.

But that's a lot of work, and the pay-off isn't usually worth it.

Because most of the people who become famous, they don't necessarily become very rich at the same time.

And that means it becomes a huge hassle to take the subway—you're so famous that everyone bugs you for autographs.

But you don't have the cash to take a taxi. It's just a nightmare.

So in New York it's better to just be New York famous, where people in your particular group know you, rather than superstar famous. That way you get the ego-boost, without all of the inconvenience.

Of course, the ideal situation would be to make enough money that you could take taxis whenever you wanted to. But I work as a poet and medievalist, and people in these professions rarely attain any kind of financial stability.

Even the most famous poets still end up taking jobs at universities as teachers, because nobody makes any money selling books of poems.

And there are "famous" medievalists, but nobody knows who they are, except for other medievalists.

But this is the story of how I changed all that. This is the story of how I became the most famous medievalist in the world, an alchemist like the used-tire port-a-potty baron.

Chapter 2

My Boethius

After we had been living together for three years, Jason started saying that he wanted to get to know me better.

The two of us were already sharing a bed, a bank account, and a wardrobe, so I didn't really know what he was talking about.

I tried to make an effort and began by discussing "The Nun's Priest's Tale," from Chaucer's *Canterbury Tales*.

It's about this rooster named Chauntecleer, and his hen-pecking chicken-wife.

But Jason didn't take the hint.

He said, "You can talk about Chaucer with Arjun. I want to hear about *you*."

So, I told him that this lady had tried to cut in line at the supermarket when I was buying pasta sauce, but Jason persisted: "I don't want to hear about your day. I want to hear about *you*, Allen."

Well, one time when I was in high school my father nearly strangled me to death, and he always used to call me a faggot whenever he caught me reading books.

I said, "I never told anyone about that. It feels like such a relief to let it off my chest."

Jason scolded: "You *did* already tell me about that!"

It was starting to feel really totalitarian, all this insistence that I have a "self" and that I should give an *account* of it. It made me want to just read Latin with my Latin teacher Arjun.

I tried citing Lacan: "The self is based upon its own lack," I quipped.

But Jason didn't relent.

Finally I had to break up with him, and move out.

For a month and a half I subsisted on Budweiser and Marlboros.

Alcoholics Anonymous didn't help, because my personality is too contrarian—whenever I'm around sober people, all I want to do is drink.

But, when I'm at a bar, abstaining makes me feel so hip and superior.

I can't help it, it's just that I like to disagree with people— that's why my father tried to murder me.

If everyone starts piling on what a bad guy Richard Nixon was, or Atilla the Hun, I'm liable to come to their defense.

It didn't help matters much that the A.A. I had gone to was a *gay* A.A.

It was all these gay guys, and they were all telling stories about how *their* fathers had tried to murder and disown *them*.

Somehow I got set up on a kind of gay A.A. date.

A friend of a friend is this guy whose name I can't tell you, and he had been married to a super-famous pop singer, and then after they divorced he came out.

I went along with him to the gay A.A.

This guy was in his 60s, and now it was his first time being gay.

I meanwhile was in my 20s and had been living with a man for three years, but I still didn't have the hang of it.

I knew that I liked penises and poetry, but that was about it.

And of course if you've ever read French theory then you know perfectly well that all these categories are "socially constructed."

Being "gay" is this historically contingent phenomenon: there literally weren't any gay people before 1869—the summer of love.

Being gay hadn't been invented yet.

This goes back to what I was saying before, about how I don't like to talk about my "self."

And that's why I would never want to say, "My name is Allen, and I'm an alcoholic."

Because all these terms of identity—e.g., "alcoholic," "homosexual," "author," "medievalist," etc.—need to be *problematized*, as Michel Foucault would put it.

They need to be put *into context*.

Anyway, going to the gay A.A. didn't help.

But I knew that I needed to get my act together, because it had gotten to where my hands were shaking all the time.

Arjun suggested that we try reading Latin together.

Arjun reads Latin every day and watches German soap operas while he has his breakfast. He's obsessed with learning languages in order to further his medievalism.

When I decided to become a medievalist I met Arjun who is also a medievalist and he said we should meet every day to read Latin together.

I had just been laid off from my job as a labor union activist, so I had plenty of free time to read Latin and to drink too much and to try to figure out how I was going to make a living reading Latin when the unemployment ran out.

Jason was a Ph.D. student in mathematics and spent all of his time sipping expensive teas and pretending to prove math theorems at a fancy café. I pictured myself doing that only with medieval poems instead of math and I would have coffee instead of tea, and I would do that while the unemployment lasted and I would try to conspire a way to continue doing it.

Arjun was going to help me if I promised to read Latin with him every day. It seemed that he was kind of lonely, and so we met each day at the Hungarian Pastry Shop on Amsterdam and 110th Street, right across from Saint John the Divine, one of New York City's neo-medieval cathedrals.

It's this great big gorgeous tacky gothic monstrosity that I absolutely love, built back in the 1920s when America's rich would spend their philanthropy dollars trying to better society, as opposed to now, when America's rich try to destroy its very foundations by funding right-wing kooks who want to abolish the government and buy everyone machine guns.

The Pastry Shop across the street has great coconut macaroons but terrible coffee.

Arjun brought with him two copies of *De consolatione philosophiae*, by Boethius—"The Consolation of Philosophy."

This wasn't the first time that literature had saved my life.

Arjun said that we could read *The Consolation* together, translating the Latin, so that I could find some *consolation* for my failed marriage.

Boethius wrote his *Consolation* in 500 AD, while he was in prison awaiting execution.

He had been sentenced to die by King Theodoric the Great, which you can look up on Wikipedia.

That was a low point for Boethius, when he really needed consolation.

You could say it was like the Anne Frank diary of that time period.

For about a thousand years, it was the most important book in Christendom.

During the Middle Ages it was translated dozens of times into every European language.

Chaucer translated it, and Queen Elizabeth I translated it.

It was even rendered into Hebrew.

It was more popular than the Bible, which technically didn't exist yet.

Today, almost nobody reads Boethius, which if you ask me is a crying shame.

Because Boethius is *so gay*.

First of all, the heroine of the *Consolation* is this great big fierce diva, whose name is Lady Philosophy.

She's a Lady, and she doesn't stand for anybody's crap.

At the beginning of the book, Boethius is crying, all alone in prison, depressed that he's lonely and loveless and is going to be killed.

Lady Philosophy descends from the heavens, *à la* Glinda the Good Witch in *The Wizard of Oz*.

The first thing Boethius notices about her is that she's wearing an amazing dress with the Greek letters Π and Θ embroidered on it—they stand for *practical* and *theoretical* philosophy.

Her dress has been torn to shreds by the hands of uncouth philosophers.

They didn't know how to treat a lady.

This is what Nietzsche meant when he asked, "What if Truth were a woman?"

Philosophers don't know what women and homos know, which is that the Truth is very complicated, and it's much more fun to wear dresses and make-up, and there's no truth nearly as interesting as a good-old fashioned lie or drag ball.

Lady Philosophy is a scathing queen and she tells Boethius: "Get over yourself!"

Which is also the point of Nietzsche's whole philosophy: suck it up and stop acting like a coward.

Then Lady Philosophy proceeds to remind Boethius about the Truth of life, which is that this earthly existence is of no consequence, compared to the higher things of God.

The book is what we in the literary business call a "pro-simetrum," meaning that it's written in alternating passages of prose and verse.

First there's an ordinary paragraph with Philosophy and Boethius just talking plainly, and then there's a poem, and it goes back and forth like that.

It's kind of like at a Broadway show: one minute it's a serious drama, the next minute everyone is singing and dancing.

One minute you're being sentenced to death, and the next thing you know: *Everything's coming up roses!*

Well, at that time Esther Crabtree had just starting teaching at Ivy League University, right up the street from the Hungarian Pastry Shop and the Cathedral, and Esther had written a whole book about Boethius.

Esther wears all kinds of luxurious dresses that zip up in the back, and a different pair of eyeglasses everyday—her glamour and her erudition, combined with her propensity to cuss like a sailor, meant that I had developed a great big crush on her, and I would always secretly call her "Lady Philosophy" behind her zipped-up back.

I started scheming to try to get a job at Ivy League University so that I could hang out with Esther.

One part of my plan was that I would consult medieval manuscripts at the Ivy League Library, so that the folks at Ivy League University would think I had a serious, academic reason for wanting to work there.

At the Ivy League Library they have an Italian manuscript from the 14th century, written on parchment.

It's a student's copy of *The Consolation of Philosophy*, and the manuscript is called Benjamin MS 4.

An Italian student from the Middle Ages wrote out the whole book by hand.

Maybe he needed consolation, too.

As I said, everyone back in the day from Chaucer to Queen Elizabeth I read the *Consolation*.

But for some reason, this particular student had written the word "penis" in the margin of one page of the manuscript.

And then, on the next page, he had written it a second time: "penis."

I thought that this was marvelous, because six hundred years later it is also a habit of mine to draw lots of cartoons of penises in the margins of my own schoolbooks.

Also, these two "penises" were written on pages where Lady Philosophy is talking about how life is inherently worth living.

She says, "Look, Boethius, at all the things around you. There are animals everyplace, and they keep reproducing. Why would they do that, unless life were good? Why would nature keep propagating itself, unless this is all worthwhile?"

Which is a pretty interesting argument, when you think about it.

Well, this medieval schoolboy had added, ingeniously, one little word.

"Penis," he wrote. And, again: "penis."

It was as if he were trying to say to Lady Philosophy and to Boethius, "Yes, life really is all right, because, if nothing else, I can still screw."

More so, he says, "I was *made* to screw."

Genitals are the proof: life isn't so bad.

Well, I don't know if I personally agree with that idea.

After all, what does a 14th-century Italian schoolboy know about anything?

But at any rate, it *is* an idea, and therefore fun to think about.

Anyhow, I didn't get accepted to Ivy League University, I think because they could tell that I'm too crude to go to a gentleman's university, but I ended up going to Underfunded Public University, and I was happy at least to have found this new medieval boyfriend in the margins of the Boethius manuscript.

And I was very happy to have read Esther's book on Boethius, because Esther says, quite rightly I think, that Boethius conceives of philosophy both as *mental*, and as *physical*.

The prose passages in the *Consolation* use logical argument to appeal to the mind, while the poems are sensuous and appeal to the body.

In case you didn't know, this is what academics do: make interpretations about other people's books.

And really, it's a radical proposition to say that philosophy is mental *and* sensual, because, as Nietzsche was trying to point out, Western Philosophy tends to ignore and even condemn the needs of the body.

You can see that very plainly in the way that Plato fetishizes the mind.

W.H. Auden has a very funny poem called "No, Plato, No," in which he says, "there's nothing I'd rather *not* be than a disincarnate spirit."

But, in fact, that's exactly what Plato wanted to be.

He wanted to be a disincarnate spirit and said that the ideal thing to be is a form without a body, without any of the mess of having to live in the world, which sometimes sounds appealing but how could you eat or read books or make love?

That's also what a lot of so-called "Christians" want to be—spirits that live entirely in the mind, without filthy bodies and genitals and butts.

Even today, that's what we're trying to do with the internet.

The internet is this way of being a person, without having to have a body.

It's like being in heaven and looking down on the world without being in it, without having to smell what James Baldwin calls "the stink of love."

But to Plato I say, with my medieval boyfriend, simply this: "penis."

That's all the proof I need.

Maybe to you it seems like I'm talking about arcane trivia.

Maybe it seems like people who died hundreds of years ago have nothing to do with anything.

First of all I would say that dead people are people, too.

If you care about democracy then you have to care about the dead.

Whenever people start saying, "think about the children!" and "we want to make a better world for our children," that's when I get really nervous because fags like me don't have children.

Instead I think it's more important to think about the dead, and what they would want the world to look like.

Second of all, this isn't trivial nonsense from the past—it's a matter of life and death.

Without Boethius, I would have drunk myself to death and very nearly did.

This is why I wish Jason could have just listened when I was trying to tell him about Chaucer, because Chaucer really is the most important thing in the world.

Poetry is all the good things like love, which poets invented, and self-development, which was first discovered in novels, and talking to other people, which you couldn't do if you didn't have poetry to tell you what to say. Poetry is what makes life possible and I won't back down on that.

But to return to what I was saying about Boethius singing songs like he's on Broadway—

This is a very different approach from other philosophers, who are so damn serious all of the time, the way that Jason was.

"I don't want to hear about your day. Or about the poetry you like. I want to hear about *you*."

"The truth, the whole truth, and nothing but the truth."

That's tyranny!

Plato hated the body and he thought that all the poets should be kicked out of society, because we make up stories that aren't true.

He just wouldn't relent in his quest for the disincarnated truth.

And some people still take that attitude.

Theodor Adorno, for example, said, "After Auschwitz, there can be no poetry."

But if you've ever read Primo Levi's *Survival in Auschwitz*, then you know that poetry saved Levi's life.

There's a part in the book, where he and another prisoner are reciting Dante together. They're in Auschwitz, which is as close to hell as you could ever get. And they recite the part of the *Inferno* where Dante and Virgil meet Ulysses.

Ulysses says:

> *Considerate la vostra'semenza:*
> *fatti non foste a viver come bruti,*
> *ma per seguir virtute e canoscenza*

"You were not born to live like a brute, but for the pursuit of virtue and knowledge!"

When they recite those lines, they remember that there are things that make life worth living, even—believe it or not—in spite of everything.

It might not be true, but it's better than nothing.

Chapter 3

Medieval Memories

Of all the cities in North America New York City is the best and San Francisco is the worst.

In San Francisco everyone is a shallow, rude, careerist jerk—just like all the people in Manhattan—only California is also all about relaxing, smoking pot, and eating organic local food.

So it's like New York only with hippy pretentions.

In New York at least, everyone's honest about being a callous liar and that way the nice people really stick out and it makes your day to meet someone who's kind and caring and genuine.

Actually, San Francisco is lovely with its pastels, its dusky purple fogs, its brilliant golden bridge, those rolling hills, the streetcars, and all the fruit is fresh and delicious and everyone you meet is polite and beautiful and not at all stuck-up like those jerks in New York, and in San Francisco you can see naked guys on the street—it's the gayest place in the world, after all.

I'm just bitter because every time I've been on vacation to San Francisco I have suffered some kind of terrible romantic catastrophe and so San Francisco is for me a landscape upon which is written my amorous devastations.

When I look at that bridge all I can see is a breakup.

Berkeley is where Jason and I said our goodbyes after living together three years and the Mission is where Philip's boyfriend caught Philip and me *in flagrante delicto*.

If you've never actually caught anyone *in flagrante delicto*, then I would really recommend it. One time I went to work at an office job I used to have before I was a medievalist and two of my coworkers were in my cubicle *in flagrante delicto*, one of them with her panties down, the other one pulling up his trousers as I came in. I immediately ran out the room through the fire exit and down the emergency stairs and straight down three blocks away from the building. Thank god I was laid off two weeks later because it was a hard secret to keep, but a secret that needed to be kept because both of them were married to other people and that was an ethical dilemma for me, but a good story to tell at cocktail parties.

That happened in Queens, by the way, and after I was laid off I never had to go to Queens again, thank goodness.

After Philip's boyfriend caught Philip and me *in flagrante delicto*, that pretty much ruined my vacation to San Francisco and likewise on a different trip to San Francisco, when Jason and I said our goodbyes in Berkeley. I never wanted to go to the Bay Area again.

After Jason and I broke up, he wanted to go to a gay bathhouse since he had never been to one before, and this was San

Francisco, the gayest place on earth, after all, and since Jason was nervous, I had to go along with him to the bathhouse. And believe me when I say there's no better way to ruin a vacation than watching your waify, geeky, four-eyed Jewish mathematician ex-boyfriend leave you behind as he goes off down the dark corridor of a pungent San Francisco bathhouse holding hands with a six-foot body-building black dude.

I left the club and walked up Telegraph Hill, which exists in a kind of a cloud where one can see the whole beautiful city in all its pastels wrapped in a light dusky purple fog—the bridge glistening in the sun reflecting off the bay and those rolling hills. It's a gorgeous landscape and I hope I never look upon it again.

In San Francisco there's a park called Union Square, but of course it's not the real Union Square, which is on 14th Street in New York City, and that is the only city for me.

But San Francisco has a Union Square, too, where there's a big obelisk and on top of that is a golden statue of the goddess Victory, which commemorates Commodore Dewey defeating the Filipinos at the Battle of Manila.

Philip was Filipino, actually, and so the monument was a great insult to him and to his people it was a horrible reminder of centuries of imperialism.

My people after all had colonized his people, and even if you're a liberal who thinks race doesn't matter, it's still a lot to take in.

Cities are like that. The monuments and streets remind you of things even if the people and events happened centuries before and you weren't even alive.

Likewise in Berkeley, the university campus is gorgeous, but who wants to look at the very park bench where you and your lover broke up?

I live in New York City, but thank goodness whenever anyone breaks my heart, it's happened when I was in San Francisco on vacation. That way, New York just reminds me of the good times.

The idea that places can help you remember specific people and events you otherwise might not remember is a very important idea that originally was developed by the Ancients and then medieval people gave it their very own twist.

Cicero tells a story about this guy named Simonides who, like me and Jason, was visiting a bathhouse one day.

Simonides had to leave the bathhouse all of a sudden to meet with a messenger.

Then the bathhouse collapsed and everyone inside of it died.

When they tried to bury the dead, no one could recognize the corpses because they were so disfigured from the collapse.

Simonides, however, remembered who everyone was based on where each of them had been sitting.

After that, Simonides developed a technique where he would create images of places in his imagination, and in those places he would put his memories. Memory houses.

Ancient orators such as Cicero used this technology to memorize entire books.

People could memorize the entire Bible just by having images of buildings and places in their minds and then filling up those places with specific memories.

I don't really ever remember anything. I just look it up on Wikipedia or Google.

But back in the day, Saint Augustine stored all his memories in what he called the "fields and palaces of his memory."

Augustine believed that God was inside him, but he couldn't figure out where for the longest time.

Then, by writing his life story (his *Confessions*), he figures out that if God is inside him, and he remembers God being there, then it must be in his memory where God lives.

So he looks into those fields and palaces and there God is.

This was an important part of medieval religion, keeping God in your memory's palaces, and medieval people very literally had palaces in their minds, all kinds of spaces like the whole city of San Francisco with each building reminding me of where Jason made a joke, or where he went off with that black dude, or where we had pie (at Alice Waters' restaurant).

Places reminded people of certain subjects, which is why "topic" and "topography" have the same prefix, because the topic is a place.

Bad love affairs are the topic that I see when I look at the landscapes of San Francisco in my memory's palaces.

Later in the Middle Ages, it wasn't just mental places that reminded people of things, it was actual places, like in Chaucer's *Troilus and Creseyde* where Troilus sees parts of the city that remind him of his former love. He rides his horse through Troy and there is the temple where he first saw Criseyde and there is the house where they first kissed and there is the corner where he heard her sing.

Like Troilus, I can't go through certain parts of San Francisco without remembering my bad relationships and that's why I've vowed never to go to San Francisco again for any reason.

I think for my next vacation I'll go to Miami or maybe I'll go to Paris.

Because even though I'm a scholar of medieval literature, I've never been to Europe.

My friend Joan just retired and moved to Paris. She's in her 70s and I think it's so inspiring that she would pick up and leave to spend the rest of her life in the city that she loves best.

Joan lived in New York most of her adult life and that's where I knew her (somehow or other, I became her computer tutor), and whenever I walk around near Ivy League University, I remember her.

When I went over to her apartment I would always offer to move the chair from the living room to her office, but she always insisted that she needed to exercise her new replacement knee, so after we had eaten lunch she would take the chair from the living room into her office, and I would sit in one chair and she in the other chair, and I gave her computer lessons, copying and pasting and sending emails which is very time-consuming for some older folks, not just because they have trouble with computers but because they insist on writing emails like they're real letters.

Joan would always fix the same lunch—that was how she paid me for the computer lessons: lentil soup with tomatoes, and a fresh salad.

The cooked tomatoes would help me prevent prostate cancer.

"You don't mind my talking about the prostate, do you?" she asked me once.

I said, "No, of course not."

"Some people do, you know."

Joan is in her 70s and so she usually hangs out with a crowd that's uptight about prostates.

Every couple of weeks Joan would call me up with a computer problem, and I'd go to her place on the Upper West Side.

Since I don't have that many friends in their 70s, and since Joan didn't have many friends in their 20s, we got along marvelously: while we ate, we would talk about all kinds of things that Joan normally couldn't talk about, as well as things that I normally couldn't talk about.

Then I'd offer to get the chair, she'd insist that she could get it—and into her office we would go, to copy and paste.

One time though, just before Joan moved to Paris, she hired this lady to come help her pack.

The lady was packing up boxes in the living room when we finished eating, and I offered to get Joan's chair.

Joan said, "Yes, please—won't you?"

To tell you the truth, I was kind of shocked.

Joan was sitting in the office when I brought in the second chair for me to sit in, and then she whispered, "I hope you understand, Allen—if she saw me getting the chair, she would think that you're a racist."

The idea hadn't crossed my mind, but I saw what Joan was getting at: for this lady to watch a 70-year old black woman fetching a chair, while a young white boy stood idly by, would certainly give the wrong impression.

"If we're going to change things," Joan said, "we have to mind appearances. That's what my mother taught me."

Joan came from a long line of black royalty with a number of famous activists, intellectuals, and statesmen in the family, and Joan herself was an esteemed professor of history, and so she knew all about academia, and sometimes at lunch would give me very good advice about my career, and I would share with her poems by William Blake about interracial love.

One time while we were eating our lentil soup, Joan said, "Medievalists, as I'm sure you're aware, have a very bad reputation. They never get along with anybody.

"Now, dear, I know you're not going to be one of *those* medievalists, but you must be careful. Academics are jealous, neurotic people—medievalists, especially—and if they see a young charming gay boy who's happy and radical, well, then, they'll feel very jealous of you and do whatever they can to cut you down.

"I hope you don't think I'm being paranoid, but that's just the way some people are. They've felt miserable through most of their careers, and they've behaved like conformists and syco-phants, so whenever they see anyone with a spine, it will just send them into a tizzy. They'll see you, and they'll feel horribly guilty about all of the compromises they've had to make, and there's nothing more dangerous than a regretful conscience.

"You really must be careful," she continued. "I knew this one medievalist who used to live in the building here. She had always been a little egocentric—most academics are—and there's nothing wrong with that, in and of itself. She was per-fectly nice, really, and we would have lunch together from time to time. But then she was invited to teach at Oxbridge, and, my, how it changed her! You know, because she was Ameri-can—the daughter of missionaries, of all things—and so for her to be invited to teach at Oxbridge, and to be a *medievalist* at Oxbridge, that really meant something. She felt that she had *arrived*. Well, she was at Oxbridge for a year, and when she came back to New York she had lost fifty pounds and her hair was blonde. I mean, really! *At her age.*

"Well, the worst part of it was, for decades she had been living here with her partner. They had a lovely apartment up-stairs. And she always bossed this poor girl about. It was like Gertrude Stein and Toklas. She did the cooking and the shop-ping and the cleaning, she even laid out her outfits. Well, I took one look at that new hairdo, and I knew right then that it was over. A week later, and what do you know? I come home from the market and the poor dear is standing down in the lobby, crying her eyes out. Just crying her eyes out! And she left her with nothing. You know, that's why same-sex marriage needs to be legalized, because after a lifetime together this poor girl was left stranded."

Joan was probably right, but where does one meet a good husband, anyway?

Definitely not in San Francisco, as I learned the hard way, and maybe not in New York City, and apparently also not in Oxbridge.

It's these places that make love stay in your memory and that's why it's so important to pick the right person to be in love with, because otherwise you ruin the place forever in your memory and can never go back to a nice place like San Francisco.

I have to be careful because I really love New York and I wouldn't want to ruin it by filling it with bad memories.

Chapter 4

The President of the Medieval Academy Made Me Cry

The President of the Medieval Academy of America made me cry because she said that I was outré and a dilettante and that I was unprofessional.

I guess I was outré because I worked in the Medieval Library and instead of wearing a collared shirt I was having an identity crisis, which I expressed by wearing a very slutty t-shirt to work everyday and tight jeans that ennobled my package.

Being outré and a dilettante is part of a long tradition among my people. It goes back through all the great homos—Oscar Wilde and Socrates, to name just two famous examples.

Even so, this insult made me cry because nobody likes to get called names, especially by their boss.

One day on the office computer I found her pedagogical philosophy written down in a Word doc.

The only time we capitalize Word is when we are referring to the incarnate logos or to the Microsoft product, which is a mystical coincidence.

My boss had written that, in order for people to learn, they first need to recognize their ignorance. So her pedagogical strategy was to make people feel as ignorant as possible so that they could learn more.

This is why she made me and all of my colleagues cry at some point or another.

Like when Susan was told her French was bad and not even to bother, or when Megan was told that everyone was disappointed in her book catalogues.

In some ways I could respect this approach because in the Middle Ages it was common to beat students when they got things wrong. The idea was that you remember pain better than pleasure—this is a biological fact caused by brain chemistry—and so hurting students helped them learn their lessons.

The only lesson I learned, however, is that the President of the Medieval Academy can shove it, because I like being outré and I'm going to be as outré as possible, because like it or not, somebody has to be the exception, and the thing is, the exception just can't try to be the rule, and so I'm not pretending to be the rule.

I'm saying up front I won't change, and if you don't like it, then I'll probably cry, anyway.

Chapter 5

My Medieval Romance

A few years ago I was reading Hannah Arendt's dissertation *Saint Augustine on Love* and sitting in Washington Square Park when I noticed a cute boy across the way.

Washington Square Park is where Jasper Johns and Robert Rauschenberg first met, so naturally I was attentive.

Augustine says it's a good thing to *use* people and love is a way of using people to get closer to God. He saw God as the proper end to all of our actions, so loving people should be a means to an end, that end being God, who is love—ta-da!

So you shouldn't enjoy people for their own sake, but only for what you can get from them, which is love.

That's Augustine for you—a very wily thinker.

Pretty soon I struck up a conversation with the cute boy.

It turned out that his name was Philip and he was working at the Brecht Society for Proletarian Revolt and because I have Marxist tendencies, we developed a rapport.

A jazz band struck up a tune and soon my new friend and I were dancing and kissing.

But Philip had to get to JFK Airport because he lived in San Francisco and his return flight was that very evening.

Well, I didn't think any more of it and went about my business writing poems and reading medieval literature.

A few years later I saw Philip on the street in New York and I knew it was meant to be.

He was on vacation again and going back that night to San Francisco.

When I went to a medievalist conference in the Midwest I decided to take a train to San Francisco from Chicago, which took three days, and I was dreaming about Philip the whole time.

When I got to San Francisco, Philip said he had a boy-friend, which he really should have told me before I left New York, but I would have gone to San Francisco anyway.

Pretty soon the thing turned into a disaster because of Philip's boyfriend finding us, and some friends of friends let me hide out in Berkeley.

I broke down in a café on Telegraph and cried, wishing that I had a mother.

My mother and I haven't spoken for about three years, which is when she burnt my library: thousands of books and a chest full of all my poems and stories and diaries.

I think of her when I'm very heartbroken and also whenev-er I do my online banking because the website asks for her maiden name as a security feature.

Ironically, my mother's maiden name is Love.

No joke: her father's name was Richard.

So my grandfather was Dick Love.

Whether or not love is important and what love is, is a good question for historians.

Beliefs and concepts go out of style or they outlive their usefulness. For example, nobody today practices the rites of Ancient Egypt, although at that time the force of those beliefs inspired slaves to build the greatest architectural structures ever built by human hands.

Moses said, "Let my people go," and his people went and their beliefs lasted and lasted and are still with us in the present.

The Egyptians, on the other hand? Their beliefs just kind of evaporated.

The Greeks did a good job ensuring their ideas would be influential over the long haul of time: everyone read Aristotle during the Middle Ages and today you have to know who Plato is in order to be a success at cocktail parties.

What do these people—the Egyptians, Greeks, Jews, all the Ancients—have in common? They weren't too interested in love.

Well of course they had love and they made love and Plato wrote his *Symposium* all about people at a cocktail party discussing love, but it wasn't that important—just a cocktail party conversation.

At a certain point Jesus came and it was like Marcel Duchamp putting a urinal in the museum, because before that everyone knew about urinals but didn't think much of them and then suddenly urinals were very important, maybe the most important.

It was that way with love, too, because before Jesus, love was a second- or even a third-rate concept and nobody paid much attention to it, but then suddenly it was the most important thing in the universe: the basis of all human relations.

I hope you don't think I'm cynical saying this. I'm really quite romantic, but part of the romance for me is knowing that love didn't always exist but had to be invented and ever since it's been the one thing that everyone agrees is very important, maybe the most important thing of all.

In the 12th century, Europeans had a new idea: why not take what Jesus invented—love—and to turn it into something a little sexier?

They mixed up Christian love with some scraps of Ancient Roman friendship literature and they turned it into *amour*.

Before that, men didn't love women, but then the Catholic Church ruled that a marriage took place only when both a man and a woman consented to that marriage.

So the religion changed to say that men and women could be in love.

Before you knew it, there were all kinds of love poems and for Europeans there really hadn't been love poems like these before.

There was the *Roman de la Rose* and the songs of the troubadours all about love and lovers and beloveds.

Before this, the best thing you could be was a celibate priest, but now the best thing to be was a married person.

Next thing you know Martin Luther says that celibacy is a sham and Henry VIII has too many wives and it's the Reformation, and everyone wants to get hitched instead of being celibate.

I honestly really prefer it, because like Noah on the Ark, I think life is a two-by-two sort of deal.

But as a homosexual, my people have never really been allowed on the Ark.

It wasn't until the 19th century when someone came up with the idea of being gay and people have been being gay ever since. I know I have.

Before the 19th century, no one could really be gay because being gay isn't just having male/male sex. It's also about being in love with a man and how was any man going to be in love with another man in the uncertain taxonomic conditions before the Industrial Revolution?

Before the Industrial Revolution, people worked at home on their farms or in cottage industries, so that the only way to make a living was with your family, and a family is a husband and a wife and kids, not two dudes or two ladies.

Only when people worked outside the home in factories could men love other men, and these men moved to cities, which everyone ever since Lot knows to be places of sin.

My point is that we live in different times and today people meet their lovers on the internet with websites that operate on the same algorithm as Amazon.com, which recommends what books you might like based on what other books you like.

So today you can order a boyfriend or girlfriend the same way you order a book—based on the website's mathematics and what you're willing to pay.

Since that's not very romantic and the alternative for me is hooking up with a stranger at a gay bar, well, when I saw Philip that second time, I thought it must be for real.

Because that's how love is supposed to work—the magical way that I was taught to believe in love.

It's a miraculous thing which Jesus himself came up with.

The first miracle he undertook was at the Wedding at Cana, turning water into wine, and his parables are all about brides and bridegrooms.

There's a medieval poem, *The Vision of Piers Plowman*, about a guy who is looking for someone named DoWell, and DoWell means living the right way, and whoever the traveler meets tells him a different story, and nobody knows where to find DoWell.

Each lover I take is another messenger, but their stories don't add up, and doing well doesn't make any sense to me.

In the *Romance of the Rose*, the God of Love commands his vassals to love and he tells them what to do.

And that's what happened to me: the God of Love told me to go to San Francisco and when it didn't work out, Love punished me by breaking my heart because I had failed his commandments.

Chapter 6

The Formation of a Persecuting Society

Everyone was talking shit about Marty again, and I had just about had it.

My colleagues and I were all driving to a conference from the Center for Medieval Studies in New York City, in a three-car medievalist caravan to Kalamazoo, Michigan.

It was a very long car ride and it took us from the most densely populated part of the country, to one of the sparsest.

In between there were a lot of pretentious conversations about literature, post-modernism, and opera, especially about Wagner's *Tristan und Isolde*—adapted from the medieval romance and performed that season at the Met—as well as sing-alongs to Boston and Freddie Mercury.

We are the champions, my friend.

We were all driving out to Kalamazoo, Michigan because once a year the University of Western Michigan hosts a big medievalist shindig.

It's an annual conference with, like, 5,000 medieval scholars, and everyone is talking about Chaucer and drinking too heavily, and—believe me—it isn't pretty.

Freddie Mercury had got me going, but then, at some point while we were passing through Ohio, everyone in the car started talking shit about Marty, and I knew it was going to be a rotten trip.

Our colleague Marty studied Burgundian castles, and Burgundian castles were the only thing he ever talked about.

That was why Marty was travelling to Kalamazoo alone via airplane, instead of being invited to join in the road trip.

He just never stopped with the Burgundian castles.

While we were in the car in Ohio, Marty was probably at the moment touching down at the Kalamazoo airport, and the unfortunate fellow traveler in the plane seat beside Marty was probably feeling very lucky to finally get off the plane, away from Marty and his incessant talk of Burgundian castles.

If you ran into Marty in the bathroom, then you would find him at the urinal talking to himself about Burgundian castles.

If Marty noticed you, then he would start talking to you, too, about Burgundian castles, even while you were pissing.

Wherever Marty went, as soon as he opened his mouth, the eyes would start to roll.

In French class, Marty would throw up his hand, and before he was called upon, he would start talking in French about Burgundian castles.

In Latin class, too, same thing: Marty would talk about Burgundian castles, in awkward Latin.

There's probably nothing more annoying than people trying to talk in Latin, which is a hard language to talk in, especially when they are talking about something as inherently annoying as Burgundian castles.

To make matters worse, these were *translation* classes and not *conversation* classes, so everyone else always spoke in English, and nobody but Marty ever talked about Burgundian castles, although when Marty talked, Marty *only* talked about Burgundian castles.

Marty also wore a fedora that was too big for him, and before he set about doing anything, he would swallow several large pills and then call his mother.

You see, Marty's obsession with Burgundian castles and his habit of making other people feel very uncomfortable—these were not just little quirks, but they were the symptoms of what people in the psychology business call "Asperger's Syndrome."

Of course, one could tell right away that Marty knew he was an *odd duck*.

He knew perfectly well that he didn't do things the *right* way, and it would have hurt him terribly, had he heard people making fun of him.

Marty had feelings, after all, even if he didn't know how to express them except by discussing Burgundian castles.

And personally I felt a lot of admiration for Marty.

To me there's nothing quite so marvelous as watching people being made to feel uncomfortable.

I just absolutely love it when someone points out: the emperor has no clothes.

And, whether he knew it or not, that was what Marty was doing, whenever he annoyed the hell out of people.

He 'pointed up' (as academics like to say) the *social constructed-ness* of the behaviors that we take as natural, as given, as the *right* way of doing things. In other words, his bad behavior just reminded us all what hypocrites we were for pretending to be civilized.

And, for doing for us that marvelous service—which is the true calling of poets and artists and thinkers and lovers and saints—Marty was roundly hated.

Meanwhile, he was also pursing an advanced degree and doing a first-rate job of it.

One of my colleagues, a mousy little historian, was saying in the back of the car, "I can't believe Marty was invited to give a talk at the conference. Whoever made that decision is definitely going to regret it."

Someone else—an expert in medieval economics—added: "I'm going to go to his talk, just so I can see how *bad* it is."

Mind you, these were highly civilized people: they were getting PhDs in medieval European history, and they liked nothing better than going to the opera and drinking the finest English teas.

But, somehow, they had gone through their lives without learning: whenever anybody is horribly weird, then really the best thing that you can do—the most polite thing that you can do—is simply to mind your own business, and to let him or her go on being weird.

It takes—if I may say so—a highly refined aesthetic sense to be able to appreciate the *beauty* in abject weirdness.

Weirdness is an acquired taste.

But then again, so is the opera.

So is English tea, and so is medievalism.

And that's what was at the heart of why everyone was persecuting Marty.

Because—let's face it—the people driving out to Kalamazoo were some of the weirdest freaks in the country—all of us obsessed with the Middle Ages and dedicating our lives to it.

So, the weirdest among all of us weirdos was getting singled out, and he was made the scapegoat.

Well, as much as I happen to care about "European Civilization"—with its operas, teas, and medieval poems—there is this unfortunate underside to our culture.

Whenever Westerners get the chance, we scapegoat and condemn, and we rape, murder, plunder, enslave, and we otherwise do what we can to oppress other people, especially if they're weird or different.

I could cite numerous examples. But this isn't a history lesson.

Well, I have this sort of bad habit of being self-righteous, so I told off all of my colleagues, and then pretended to take a nap the rest of the car ride.

What I was *really* doing (instead of napping) was thinking about someone named R.I. Moore.

Several years ago, R.I. Moore wrote a very interesting book called *The Formation of a Persecuting Society*, about persecution in the Middle Ages, and about how ever since the Middle Ages, Westerners have been gung-ho about oppressing people.

The Middle Ages are, quite famously, a time of dungeons and torture, and whenever the *New York Times* writes about Abu Ghraib or some such, they always use the word "medieval," which, as a medievalist, I take very personally, but the point still stands: something about our culture is really fucked up, and things got particularly bad during the medieval period.

At that time it was common for weirdos to be labeled as heretics, and then to be murdered.

Also, Jews and fags.

The subtitle of Moore's book is, *Authority and Deviance in Western Europe, 950-1250*, and it's all about the particular social conditions that led to witch-hunts, to fag-burnings, to pogroms, to the Inquisition.

For the last, like, 70 years, Westerners have been asking themselves—with good reason—what the hell is wrong with us, that we have done these wicked things?

Why are we so evil?

Asking that question is kind of a new thing.

For a long time, people took it for granted that evil didn't actually even exist.

The great medieval Christian philosophers—for example, Augustine and Boethius—they maintained that evil is not a *thing*, not a positive force.

How could God make anything that was evil?

Well, He couldn't, because everything that He does is just right.

So, if God didn't make anything bad, what is all this stuff we consider to be "evil"?

Augustine and Boethius had an ingenious answer: the stuff that looks evil to us, is actually just stuff that isn't very good.

Medieval people said, evil doesn't exist.

Mind you, this didn't stop them from killing fags, Jews, witches, and weirdos.

But, then, in the 20th century, something happened that changed the way we think about evil.

I think you know what I'm referring to.

And ever since, philosophers have been wondering why Westerners are so wicked.

This is what people in the philosophy business call "radical evil."

It's the idea that evil *does* exist, as an actual thing, and that we have to come to terms with it.

That's why R.I. Moore wrote his book, to try to figure out

what happened, when somewhere along the way, Westerners became so cruel that we could enslave entire continents, destroy entire cultures, and murder and maim and steal whatever stood in our way.

R.I. Moore says that Europeans weren't really all that bad, until something changed in the eleventh century, and since then persecution has been a defining characteristic of our culture.

What happened, he argues, is that this period saw the rise of a class of bureaucrats—clerks—who found it in their own interests to scapegoat others, in order to advance their own power.

Hannah Arendt in the 1950s similarly suggested that evil is "banal," and that the Holocaust happened simply because people in the genocide business were trying to get promotions.

It must just be my self-righteous streak kicking in again, but I felt pretty sure that's what was happening with Marty.

Everyone just wanted to put Marty down, because then there would be less attention put on them, and how weird *they* were.

So eventually I decided to ditch the conference and explore the Midwest, where I'd never been before. I took a train to Chicago and another medievalist was on the train and we sat together.

Tim studied monasticism, all those dudes flagellating themselves.

When two homos get together, it's really remarkable how there's automatically a sense of belonging.

Like when I walk through Greenwich Village, I can just tell who's gay and they can tell I am, too, and it's not just because we're checking each other out.

We *are* checking each other out, but it's something even

more primal than sex.

It's about survival—we try to find others like us, to stick together and protect one another, because we know what the world is capable of doing to us if we're not careful.

Well, Tim and I didn't really know each other, but we hit it off right away, talking about all kinds of things: monks, Slavoj Zizek, medieval conferences, opera, how academics can be cruel jerks who make fun of people, and politics.

Being gay is a kind of politics unto itself, and we discussed that a little bit.

About how there are some gay folks, who are really happy with the "progress" being made.

But there are just as many gay folks who think that "Don't Ask/Don't Tell" was a non-issue from the start.

Why would anyone want to join the military, anyway?

All the military does is kill people.

Better to be a hairdresser.

And why would anyone want to get married?

Marriage always ends in divorce, so why not just play around?

Well, there are many sides to every issue, and for academics, that's our bread and butter—to look at things from every angle.

So I said to Tim, "Yes I'm very glad things are getting a little better, but I have to wonder sometimes, isn't there something that's lost, when you get found?"

That was a line from a favorite book of mine, *The Queer Child*, by Katherine Bond-Stockton.

Bond-Stockton says: "Something is lost in being found."

And I think that's a very eloquent way of putting it.

Tim said, "Yes, but I'm not in favor of all this barebacking."

I wasn't really thinking about barebacking, I was talking about something existential.

Gay people really used to be a whole lot crazier, but now, thanks to AIDs, that's over.

Straight people, of course, have unprotected sex all of the time, probably even more often than gay people do.

But gay people run into more problems with that, because there aren't as many of us, and statistically we're more likely to have you-know-what, and so it just ends up that there's a bigger risk.

It's not anything to do with anything, that's just how it is.

That's the way the numbers work out.

But there is something that's lost in being found.

I just don't know what it is, exactly.

Well, Tim and I hugged goodbye when we got to Chicago, then I looked up my old friend, Maggie Magid, and we had szechuan.

We caught up and I told her about the conference and she told me about her new life in Chicago, selling beautiful thrift clothes online, and then at some point during dinner I asked her how Toné was.

Toné was this guy we'd gone to college with in New York who, last I heard, had moved back to Chicago.

Maggie told me Toné was dead.

He had gotten kicked out of college because as an art project, he had tried to kidnap the professor.

Then he fucked around for a few years working odd jobs.

Then he got HIV.

And now he was dead.

I didn't know people in the U.S. still died from AIDS, but here he was, another 26-year old faggot like me, only I was alive, and he was dead.

Well, I didn't know what to do, but all of a sudden I sure as hell wished I wasn't in the Midwest, or in the Middle Ages, either.

Chapter 7

The Medieval Heart is Like a Penis

I had noticed the scars, but didn't know their meaning. I didn't see the scars as scars, didn't know what had caused them, didn't know something was missing.

Then, at ten years of age, I read Genesis and asked my grandmother what the word "circumcision" meant.

She became very embarrassed, but she finally told me.

At last, here was a book that talked about my favorite topic—penises!

Much more fun than the Hardy Boys!

I read and reread the sex law chapter in Leviticus.

But why had this been done to me? Was it God's merciless trick, like when he made me different than the other boys?

In Christian theology, the heart is like a penis: Saint Paul writes that men don't need to get circumcised, because they can be "circumcised on their hearts."

Like a penis, a heart can be soft.

And it can become hard, like when God hardened the heart of the Pharaoh.

A Christian's heart can have a mouth, too, like when Saint Augustine in his *Confessions* celebrates "the mouth of my heart, which God taught to sing!"

He says, "circumcise my lips, oh Lord!"

The heart is a penis, and a mouth, and a heart, all at the same time—three-in-one! Father and the Son, Holy Ghost—auto-fellatio of consubstantial three-way.

❦

The Grinch, who stole Christmas, cannot experience Christian love, because his member is so minute.

"His heart is two sizes too small."

The Grinch is a most peculiar bachelor; he's an outsider and a pariah, living alone in a cave (like a homo in a closet).

The Grinch hoards material goods (typical, Freud wrote, of the anal personality), and he shoves them up the chutes the wrong way.

Usually the yuletide season involves sending presents *down* the chimney, but the Grinch stuffs things *up* the chimney—much to his grinch-ish delight.

The Grinch tries to "keep Christmas from coming."

He steals all of the Whos' presents and "stuffs all the bags, one by one, up the chimney," and "then he stuffed all the food up the chimney with glee. / 'And now!' grinned the Grinch, 'I will stuff up the tree!'"

"Grinch-ish-ly humming," he gleefully says, "Pooh-pooh to the Whos!"

But, thankfully, the Grinch is touched at last by the spirit of Christmas: he realizes that, despite his best efforts:

He hadn't stopped Christmas from coming!

It came!

Somehow or other, it came just the same!

Somehow or other, the pooh-poohing chimney-stuffer is faced with the inarguable logic of Christmas. At last, his small heart grows big.

The Christian heart, like a queer heart, is not a *normal* heart.

As W.H. Auden wrote in "September 1, 1939," the normal heart is one that craves romantic—rather than Christian—love:

What mad Nijinsky wrote
About Diaghilev
Is true of the normal heart;
For the error bred in the bone
Of each woman and each man
Craves what it cannot have,
Not universal love
But to be loved alone.

The normal heart is the one that wants "what it cannot have."

The normal heart is full of illicit desires—it wishes "to be loved alone."

Christians, on the other hand, believe in a universal love.

Unlike Christian love, gay love is normal: the gay Russian dancers Vaslav Nijinsky and Serge Diaghilev are, as Auden writes, "crude" in their normality.

The normality of gay love is not at all virtuous, but rather is proof of its insufficiency. Holier, more perfect, is the abnormal heart of the Christian. Compared to the crude, normal homos, Christians are the fags.

So, in Larry Kramer's *The Normal Heart*, the character based on Kramer, Ned Weeks, is betrayed by his friends, and therefore he is Christ-like.

But Ned is finally accepted by his brother as "normal."

And Ned himself does not die from the plague.

In the end, the play resists any Christian analogies.

Gays really do have normal hearts.

The heart is an empty vessel, ready to receive God's love: "Have you accepted Jesus into your heart?"

Only if he uses protection.

"Circumcision is that of the heart, in the spirit, and not in the letter."

Saint Paul means that Christianity is a posture of privileging the figurative over the literal.

The Christian is not marked on the body, but in the spirit.

Paul describes an aesthetic sensibility: it is not the outer penis that counts, but the penis inside one's heart.

Just as, literally speaking, I am a man (I check the box on the census form).

But, inwardly, I am something other.

Not "this sex which is not one," but not the other one, either.

❧❧❧

King Solomon writes, "Let him kiss me with the kiss of his mouth!" (*The Song of Songs*).

For the medieval theologian, Saint Bernard of Clairvaux, to be "kissed by the kiss of his mouth" is not to be kissed by a simple mouth, but to be "kissed by a kiss."

There's a redundancy in Solomon's poem, because a kiss is always a "kiss of the mouth."

Bernard believes that the redundancy indicates how the kiss exists, apart from the kissers.

The kisser and the kissed make between them a third entity, the kiss itself: "the kiss that is common both to him who kisses and to him who is kissed."

The kiss is the kiss that kisses both kisser and kissed. This kiss is the Holy Ghost, the "imperturbable peace of the Father and the Son, their unshakable bond, their undivided love, their indivisible unity."

This is what Christ meant when he said: "For where two or three are gathered together in my name, there am I in the midst of them."

The bond between two Christians creates between them the bond itself, a third force, the Holy Spirit.

Like the so-called "gay community."

When I love my beloved, I love him not *despite* being gay, but *because* he is gay.

I love him more than any other, for the very reason that we are otherwise despised.

The source of our stigma is the grounding of our love.

Gayness is our shared lot, our mutual heritage, the mark that brands us both.

It is the kiss that we kiss, when we kiss one another.

Chapter 8

Jilted Again

I went to hear my favorite poet when he was reading his poems at a bookshop in Greenwich Village.

He's a very famous poet, which is like being a famous medievalist, where nobody knows who the hell you are except a small crew of weirdos who have insatiable crushes on all things medieval.

In the middle of the poet's reading, one of the audience members had a seizure.

It wasn't, like, grand mal, but it was serious enough to stop the show.

The poet meanwhile kept his composure.

He's really a pro like that.

Afterward, I tried flirting with him by saying that I admired one of the poems he read.

It's about seeing a big dildo in the trash can on the street corner while the poet goes into the bank to cash a birthday check. When he comes out, children are kicking the dildo down the sidewalk. Happy Birthday.

In his poem, the poet had quoted a line from *The Canterbury Tales*: "and bathed every veyne in swich licour."

I told him that I admired his medieval reference.

"Thanks," he said. "Are you a Chaucerian?"

"No," I said, "but I'm a medievalist."

He said, "That's pretty much the same thing."

That hurt me as bad as if I were a Dominican, and he had called me Puerto Rican.

I broke up with him after that, and I returned all of his books to the library.

Chapter 9

My Orpheus

Even though my boyfriend Jarret had broken up with me, I still made him an elaborate Christmas present.

I translated a medieval poem called *Sir Orfeo* from Middle English into rhyming Modern English couplets, and I dedicated the translation to Jarret.

I first met Jarret on the subway one day while I was reading *Sir Orfeo*.

His started gazing at me and I blushed and hid behind the book.

Blushing isn't something I ordinarily do. It's only happened to me that once.·

After I met Jarret I was thinking about the blushing girl eagle in Chaucer' *Parliament of Fowles* and about how the point of the poem is, don't even try talking about love because once you start, you can never stop talking and you'll never quite hit the mark.

I fell in love with Jarret, but if you asked me why, I couldn't tell you.

Chaucer says, "The life so short, the craft so long to learn," meaning that love is a very difficult subject of study and as someone who professionally studies love poetry, I can assure you it's true.

One thing I wonder about is the theory of love and the practice of love and how they don't match up that well all the time.

Blushing is a kind of practice, but what does it mean?

Writing a love poem is part of the practice of love, I thought, and so I wrote a translation of *Sir Orfeo* for Jarret, even though he had broken up with me.

Sir Orfeo is about the Orpheus myth in which Orpheus's wife Eurydice is taken into hell and Orpheus goes to get her.

The god of the Underworld says Orpheus can take Eurydice back, as long as he doesn't look behind him as he exits Hell.

For whatever reason, Orpheus looks back, and Eurydice disappears.

However, in the medieval version, *Sir Orfeo*, Orfeo and Eurydice return to earth and everything is 'happily every after.'

The moral of the classical version is that you shouldn't disobey the gods, and you shouldn't barge straight into Hell like Rambo, guns a'blazing, trying to get your wife back from the Devil.

Medieval people valued patience and contemplation, and love and forgiveness, and this is why Orfeo just waits patiently for many, many years before he is invited to Hell, and when he gets there, he is humble.

I translated this for Jarret, both because I was reading it when we met, and because I still loved him and hoped that I could retrieve him back from the Underworld of being broken up.

I hoped that, by being patient and humble and maintaining my love for Jarret, I could win him back.

But then Jarret told me that he had been HIV+ the whole time we were together and that he'd been keeping it a secret from me, and this was why he broke up with me. And I couldn't be patient anymore because, after all, I'm not a medieval saint, I'm just some guy who meets men on the subway and writes poems for them.

Chapter 10

Medieval Literacy

In the Middle Ages hardly anybody could read or write. Maybe only, like, 10% of the people in Europe could.

Things still got done and everyone heard good stories because the people who could read, would read aloud to others.

Today everyone in the U.S. learns to read, and if you have a professional job then you have to write a lot.

If you're a banker, you write bank statements, and if you're a scientist, you write science articles, and in movies about office workers, the boss is always asking someone, "Did you remember to file that report?"

Which gives me the impression that people have to file a lot of reports, no matter what their job is.

Even though there is so much writing to be done, it's very hard for professional writers to make a living.

For example, if you write for a news outlet on the internet, like the *Huffington Post*, you probably write for free.

Or if you're like me, maybe you have a degree in literature and you spend all your time writing, but nobody pays you for it.

This is why people who study literature for a living should band together and refuse to teach other people how to write.

I teach a literature class, but I don't want to teach my students to write papers, because how will I make a living?

My bread and butter is writing and if it were the Middle Ages, then I would be knighted for my learning, but instead I make subsistence wages working at an underfunded public university, and honestly sometimes I would rather be knighted than try to further democracy, although democracy might be a fair tradeoff for not making enough money to pay the rent.

Chapter 11

My Cloud of Unknowing

One time I was in this cult, and it was a very positive experience.

Of course, there were also many weird things about it.

For example, they had this belief that if you gave all your money to the cult, then that would change your karma.

And everyone worshipped this chubby Japanese businessman who was called the 'Sensei.'

And, in many ways, it was demeaning and repressive and unbearable.

I knew perfectly well from the beginning that it was a cult, but that didn't stop me.

No, sir, not for a second.

With my ex-boyfriend Drew, it was the same thing: I knew that he was a lying narcissist, and dumb as a brick.

Even after Drew lied to me and to all of my friends and said that he was nominated for a Grammy Award, I still kept persisting in trying to make a relationship with him work.

He was the person who got me involved with the cult.

I suppose it was his charming demeanor that won me over—his warm Jamaican smile and his psychopathic ability to manipulate me into doing anything he asked.

A few dates in with Drew, I woke up at his apartment, and he said he was going to start *chanting*.

He said he was a Buddhist, and that he chanted every morning.

He chanted this mantra over and over, sometimes for hours.

Chanting was supposed to change your karma.

Well, like most every young working-class white guy, back when I was a disgruntled adolescent, I had read the Beat poets, Kerouac and Ginsberg, and they turned me on to pot, and khakis, and Buddhism.

So chanting some mantra wasn't a big stretch of the imagination for me to wrap my mind around.

I got right down there on the floor with Drew and started chanting it, over and over and over again.

Pretty soon, I was going to meetings, and it was a lot like A.A., only instead of everyone crying about how they had ruined their lives with alcohol, everyone was smiling and talking about how they were overcoming their bad karma.

The secret was, to chant this mantra.

And to donate money to the Sensei.

Usually, at the meetings, there were cookies, and sometimes whole buffets, so it wasn't without its comforts.

As a medievalist, I thought it all made a certain amount of sense because of this medieval book called *The Cloud of Unknowing*.

The *Cloud* talks about how there's a cloud between us and God.

The "cloud" prevents us from seeing Him.

But all we have to do is chant a mantra and the words will strike the cloud and make it dissipate.

So religious people in the Middle Ages were doing something pretty similar to what I and my Buddhist boyfriend were doing in Brooklyn.

You just pick one word, and you say it again and again.

The Cloud of Unknowing recommends that you pick a word like "Love," or "God."

But you can also pick a word like "Bad." It doesn't matter what the word means, as long as you say it over and over.

Chanting a mantra is a kind of hypnotism, and it does make you feel good, no matter what the words are.

But that is precisely where I ran into trouble, because it turned out everyone in the cult honestly believed the nonsense that they were spewing, so I couldn't keep pretending. It wouldn't have been fair to them.

It turns out that this is an enduring problem of history— that, on the one hand, everything seems interesting: you read a weird book like *The Cloud of Unknowing* and you think it has such a cool title and it's a marvelous idea, but where you go wrong, on the other hand, is when you forget that people actually believed this kooky shit, and it's not just a story—it's a religion.

You might enjoy that book like you enjoy a play, watching it for an hour and believing it, but then going home and knowing it's not true.

But for some people, it's real life.

And people like that—you probably shouldn't live with them.

Which is why, one weekend, when Drew went on a trip to hear Sonic Youth, he must have picked up some bad karma, because he came home and all his stuff was packed up in the lobby of our building and the locks had been mystically changed.

Sometimes you have to change your karma.

But the past is not something you *always* have to live with. You can visit the past whenever you want, but nobody expects you to believe in it or love it, especially when it turns out to have been a miserable place full of liars who also believed in bad ideas.

Chapter 12

The Post-medieval Unconscious

I started seeing a shrink on the Upper West Side whose name is Dr. Isolde.

When I said I was a medievalist she tried to reassure me.

"My maiden name is Katz—like the deli."

Her name bothered me because of the medieval story, *Tristan and Isolde*.

"I hope this doesn't mean I'm Tristan," I said.

"'Tristan' means 'the sad one'," I said as I laid down on the couch, complaining to Dr. Isolde.

I was dating two men with practically the same names, Kibway and Keelay. That's the kind of situation you need a shrink for.

There's that medieval myth about the two knights, Amis and Amiloun. They are BFFs and look exactly alike and were born on the same day. Amiloun can't appear at his own wedding (he's got good reasons), and Amis marries Amiloun's wife for him. Because friends do that sort of thing for each other in the Middle Ages.

But God punishes Amis with leprosy.

But then Amiloun murders his own children and everything works out, because he uses their blood to magically bathe and cure his friend.

And then the children are restored to life miraculously. because stuff like that happened in the Middle Ages.

Meanwhile, I met Jarret while I was in the middle of reading *Sir Orfeo* on the L train and that's why I broke up with both Kibway and Keelay.

Oddly enough Jarret and I have the same birthday, July 14th, which is also Bastille Day, and I always take that for a sign—romanticism gone overboard.

Dr. Isolde says it's fine to be convinced of one's own genius, but just don't announce it to your colleagues.

I tell her that my relationship with medievalism isn't working, as it's too tough trying to keep track of so much meaning.

I walk downtown after therapy and go through Rockefeller Center, with Franz Kline in the window at Christie's, and it's next to the *Today* show, so you can see Matt Lauer.

People formerly believed in things—at least, they thought they did and they used lots of chrome back then to prove it: a *beaux art* goddess named Thought adorns the GE building.

GE is a fake company that the government keeps pretending is real—the same as me wanting to believe in art, and apparently also this thing with Jarret, too.

Maybe it's time I see what's going on and watch this show *Madmen* everyone is talking about.

Meanwhile, it's Christmas and New York is the city that invented Christmas.

After we have sex, he says it's like paying the rent.

Dr. Isolde likes my new villanelle, "The Origins of Totalitarianism."

It's about Hannah Arendt, who had written her dissertation on Saint Augustine's theory of love, but that was after she changed advisers from her badboy Nazi paramour Heidegger to the more sensible choice Jaspers.

One of my students said it's judgmental to hate anyone, and you have to see where they're coming from, even with Hitler.

This is something about which I'm quite conservative.

My ex-boyfriend Drew had seen a YouTube video in which Marina Abramovic announced, "Art must be beautiful."

He kept repeating it to everyone, like it was a revelation.

This is the feeling I get when I look at the Mérode Altarpiece (a great late-medieval pious triptych of the Annunciation and Joseph the Carpenter), myself refracted back upon myself, the triptych figuring me for me—I'm the patron and I'm praying to the Virgin and I am the Virgin and the Angel is annunciating this to me, in much the same way as when Tristan, who has no father, discovers all of a sudden that he has three different fathers and all of them are dead.

Dedication

You may have noticed that this book is dedicated to J.H.

This is the same Jason that I have mentioned several times as one of my ex-boyfriends.

Jason and I haven't spoken for years.

But we work at the same university in the same building on the same floor.

Sometimes I run into him in the men's room and I blurt out awkward things like, "I like your hair," which is one of the worst things one can say in a men's room.

Jason never responds.

So dedicating this book to him is an act of literary revenge.

The dedication is an entirely unwanted honor.

But so far, there haven't been any court orders against it.

You see, when we were together, Jason was always insisting that I should learn to communicate better and to tell him more about myself and my way of thinking.

He said he wanted to get to know me better.

But he was a terrible listener and uncommonly dismissive.

Naturally, then, I didn't know how to respond.

But I did think at that time that, some day, I might write a little memoir, explaining my life and my philosophy—my 'way of thinking.'

But after five years apart from somebody—Jason—with whom I had a dysfunctional relationship, why would I go to the trouble of dedicating a book to him?

Why not use that poetic capital to invest in a viable current relationship?

I could dedicate this book, say, to my current boyfriend, who is nice and who is a good listener.

But, no, it's for Jason.

Why?

The answer, I'll tell you plainly, is this: that's part of the sensibility of the medievalist.

I dwell in the past.

The past is as good a time as any.

This is a kind of Walt Whitman-esque, uber-expansive, groovy democratization of time—all times are just as important as the other times. And we medievalists really get this.

The New Agers like to tell people: "live in the moment."

But the moment isn't anything at all—practically speaking, it doesn't exist, it's just the passing away of the future into the past.

And the past is where all of the interesting things happened.

This attitude of mine is something I don't think Jason could have ever understood.

In those days, we lived in Washington Heights, in New York City.

That's where the Cloisters Museum is. The Cloisters Museum was put together with pieces of medieval monasteries from France that were pillaged by the Rockefellers and brought over, stone-by-stone, to New York City.

There's even a chapel that holds the mummy of a dead saint in a glass box, just like in medieval literature.

That was sheer heaven for me to see the relics of a saint, just like in a story by Chaucer, and to also see in the park by the museum lots of gay dudes having sex in the well-manicured shrubbery.

I would walk by on my way to the museum to do my very professional medievalist work, and on the way, I would always see a penis or two, and that really makes my day—not sexually, but as an historian.

Formerly in Manhattan, in the 60s and 70s, you couldn't go into Central Park without seeing gay dudes giving blowjobs, but it's not like that anymore.

Now all of the public sex has disappeared from the city, and it only happens in the park by the Cloisters Museum.

In a way, my whole life with Jason in Washington Heights was a throwback to a different time—the saint's corpse and the pillaged monasteries and the dudes in the shrubbery.

It reminded me of some memory that I had read about in a poem, someone recounting someone else's memory, which I can now remember for their having remembered it in the first place, like a medieval book that was stolen from Europe and recreated in Manhattan.

And that's why this book you are now holding is dedicated to Jason, because in some time *back there*, this is all still important, even if he wants to forget that it happened. And because I'm a medievalist. And the 'back there' is where we live.

At eight years old, **A.W. Strouse** was so titillated by the Old Testament that he built a sacrificial altar on his parents' front lawn. He prayed that God would fill him with the Word, but no divine inspiration was forthcoming. Instead, Strouse's earthly father spanked him heartily for having killed the grass. Ever since, Strouse has been attempting to create a kind of faggy, Christian mysticism through his practice as a poet and through his work as a medievalist. He believes that grace isn't possible without one's first having gone through hell, so he celebrates the campy and the dimwitted as modes of apophatic spirituality. He is the author of *Retractions and Revelations* (Jerk Poet, 2014) and *Thebes* (Jerkpoet, 2015), and he co-operates the Ferro Strouse Gallery. He holds a B.A. from The New School and an M.A. in Medieval Studies from Fordham University. He lives in Brooklyn and teaches medieval poetry at the City University of New York, where he is writing his doctoral dissertation on literary theories of the foreskin.

Printed in Great Britain
by Amazon